Thomas Edison
and the Pioneers of
Electromagnetism

Elizabeth R. C. Cregan, MDE

Physical Science Readers:
Thomas Edison and the Pioneers of Electromagnetism

Publishing Credits

Editorial Director
Dona Herweck Rice

Creative Director
Lee Aucoin

Associate Editor
Joshua BishopRoby

Illustration Manager
Timothy J. Bradley

Editor-in-Chief
Sharon Coan, M.S.Ed.

Publisher
Rachelle Cracchiolo, M.S.Ed.

Science Contributor
Sally Ride Science

Science Consultants
Jane Weir, MPhys

Teacher Created Materials

5301 Oceanus Drive
Huntington Beach, CA 92649-1030
http://www.tcmpub.com
ISBN 978-0-7439-0576-3
© 2007 Teacher Created Materials, Inc.

Table of Contents

The Wizard of Menlo Park 4

The Early Years 6

A Team Effort 8

Harnessing the Power of Electricity 12

On the Radio 14

Pioneers of Electromagnetism 18

Oersted's Discovery 22

Faraday's Unified Force 24

Astronomer: Margaret Kivelson 26

Appendices 28

    Lab: Create an Electromagnet 28

    Glossary 30

    Index 31

    Sally Ride Science 32

    Image Credits 32

The Wizard of Menlo Park

Thomas Edison is one of the most famous inventors of all time. His inventions are still very important in today's world.

Edison worked with a team of scientists. They invented something new every 2 weeks for 45 years. Their inventions are all around us. Edison's most famous **invention** is the light bulb.

How did Edison invent so many new things? People joked that he must be a magician. They nicknamed him the Wizard of Menlo Park.

By age 23, Edison had invented a light bulb that lasted a long time. He also invented the power grid. A power grid gives **electricity** (uh-lek-TRIS-uh-tee) to homes and businesses. The phonograph, movie camera, copy machine, and **alkaline** (AL-kuh-line) storage battery are all Edison's inventions.

Edison's lab

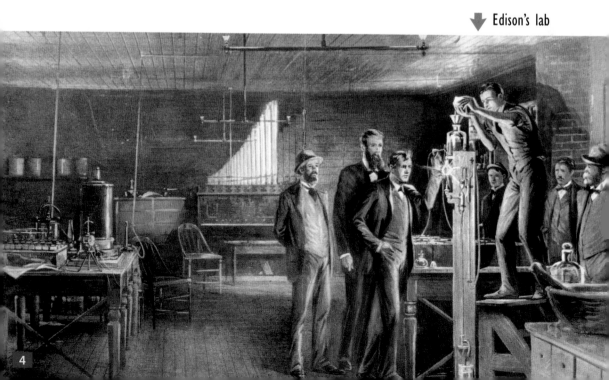

Patents

When an inventor creates something new, he or she wants to be sure no one else will use his or her idea. Inventors apply to the government for a document called a **patent**. A patent protects an inventor's ideas. Thomas Edison holds the record for the most patents for new inventions. He holds over 1,000 in the United States!

← Edison as a young man

She Did It First

Mary Dixon Kies was the first woman to receive a U.S. patent. She patented her method of weaving straw with silk. Her method was used to improve the making of hats. (At that time, nearly everyone wore hats.) Kies received her patent on May 5, 1809.

← The mimeograph machine was one of Edison's early inventions.

The Early Years

Thomas Edison was born in Milan, Ohio, in 1847. As a young boy, Edison loved to study new things. He liked to read, too.

Edison started school late because of an illness. He did not do well in school. His mind wandered. His teachers did not think he was very smart. So, Thomas' mother took him out of school and helped him learn at home.

When Edison was a teen, he left home and traveled around the country. He worked as a **telegraph** operator. He was partially deaf, but this helped him block out noise. He couldn't hear the operators sitting next to him.

Edison worked long hours. He only slept four or five hours a night. But he loved to take catnaps. When he had his own lab, if anyone ever visited him at work, they might see him sleeping on top of a table!

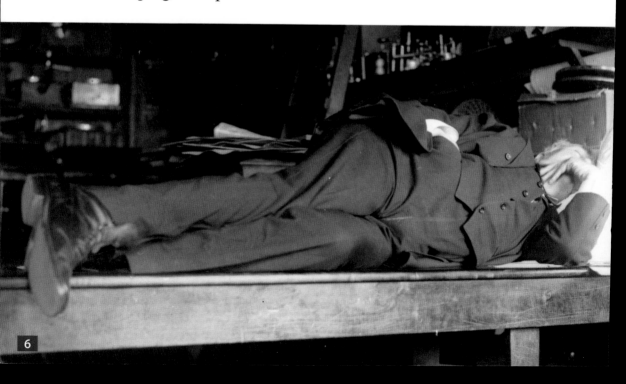

The Morse kids, Dash (above) and Dot (right)

Morse Kids

Telegraph operators used a language called **Morse code**. Their job was to use this code to send electronic messages. The operator would tap short bursts of electricity called dots and dashes. Different groups of dots and dashes stood for letters of the alphabet. Later, when he had children, Edison nicknamed two of his children Dot and Dash after the Morse code.

Working on the Railroad

Mattie "Ma" Kiley was one of the first female telegraph operators to work for the railroads. The railroad system had to communicate. Dispatchers used the telegraph to share information. Kiley worked for the railroads until 1942.

Mattie "Ma" Kiley

Edison was comfortable at Menlo Park.

Edison began his career as an inventor in New Jersey. He wanted to invent things that would help other people. Also, he tried to invent things that people would want to buy. This made him good at business, too.

Edison liked to work with other inventors and scientists. In fact, he invented a new way for scientists to work together. First, he would make a sketch in his notebook. Then, he would give it to his team of inventors. They would start to build the invention that Edison had sketched. Edison would work with them until the invention was finished. This became the way that many scientists today do research.

The invention of the phonograph in 1877 made him famous. People were soon wondering what he would think of next.

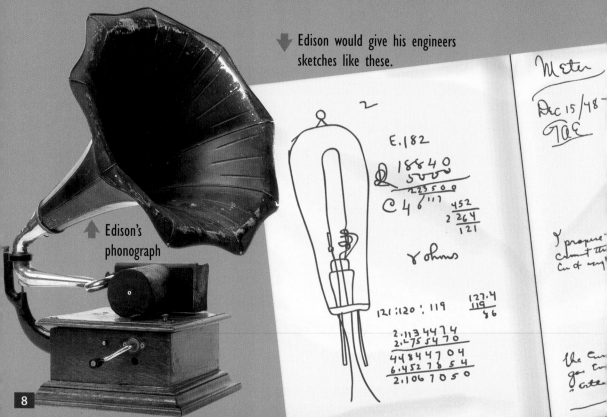

Edison would give his engineers sketches like these.

Edison's phonograph

Today's Engineer

Ellen Ochoa (oh-CHOH-uh) is an electrical engineer working in the United States. She has three patents for her own inventions. She is also an astronaut for NASA.

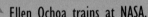 Ellen Ochoa trains at NASA.

▼ Edison and his team of engineers

Edison's Team

Edison worked hard day and night. People came from all over the world to work with him. Like him, they would work long hours for days and only break when they had a solution. During their breaks, they would often sing along to organ music. Edison kept a large organ along one wall of his lab!

Thomas Edison was the first to create a light bulb that would last a long time. At that time, homes were mainly lit with oil or gas lamps.

Edison and his team worked for many months to invent a better light bulb than the ones that already existed. One group worked on the glass part of the light bulb. Another group tried to find the right material to burn inside the bulb. They tested more than 1,600 materials, including spider webs and human hair. They were determined to find the answer.

◄ Edison's light bulb

In 1879, they finally found something! Edison discovered that cotton thread could burn for 13 hours. The thread was baked and turned into carbon. Then the carbon was put inside a glass bulb. When the bulb was connected to an electrical **current**, it glowed.

Now, people had a light bulb that they could use in their homes.

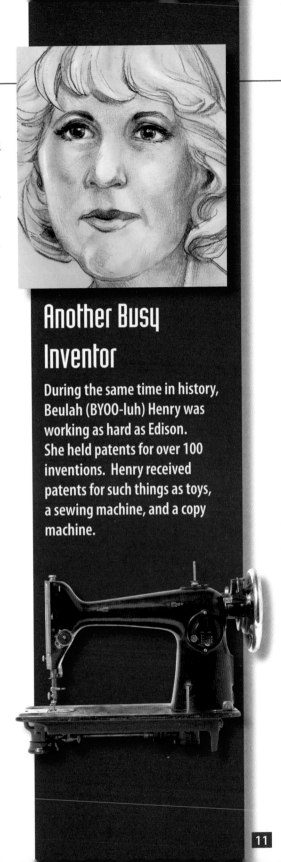

Another Busy Inventor

During the same time in history, Beulah (BYOO-luh) Henry was working as hard as Edison. She held patents for over 100 inventions. Henry received patents for such things as toys, a sewing machine, and a copy machine.

▼ Who knew that cotton would be the key to a better light bulb?

▲ Edison punching a time clock at General Electric

Of course, light bulbs are useless without electricity to run them. Edison started working right away to invent many other things needed to create the electricity to light these bulbs. Edison wanted to be the first person to bring electricity into people's homes.

Edison worked on a way to make electricity and get it out to paying customers. He invented **generators** (JEN-uh-ray-ters), fuses, and lighting fixtures in order to do it.

Edison figured out how to measure the amount of electricity people used. He wanted to be able to send people a bill! Edison also promised the world that he would light up the city of New York one day.

For two years, Edison worked on this idea. In 1882, Edison made parts of New York City glow with electricity. This inspired him to start his own electric company. He called it General Electric. GE, as it is often called, still exists today.

⬇ General Electric Company, New York, 1907

Electrical Engineer or Electrician?

Electrical engineers (EE) design and build everything from radar to DVD players. They design circuits (SIR-kuhts) for stereo equipment and video games. They also design computer systems. But why can't an **electrician** do these things? EEs and electricians get different training. Also, they focus on doing different kinds of work. EEs must go to college to study. Electricians learn by working with other experienced electricians. Electricians spend most of their time wiring buildings during construction. They build and repair electrical systems. Both EEs and electricians do important and needed work.

On the Radio

Thomas Edison inspired many other people because of his work. Nikola Tesla was one such person. Tesla was an inventor and an engineer. He was the first person to file a patent for basic radio. He also invented a radio-controlled boat.

Tesla came to America from southern Europe, landing in New York City in 1884. He wanted to meet his hero, Thomas Edison. Edison hired Tesla to work at his electric company.

At first, Tesla did easy jobs for Edison. Then he started to figure out some hard problems. Tesla believed he could make Edison's lighting system better. Wires crossed the streets of New

Nikola Tesla was a Serb. Today, there is a whole nation called Serbia, but Tesla was actually born in what is now Croatia.

York City. This was because the electricity being sent to customers was **direct current**, or DC. This type of electricity was cheap to produce. But it could only travel short distances. It was also very dangerous to have so many wires overhead.

Tesla had an idea.

Telephone and telegraph lines in ➡ 1891 New York City

◀ An antique radio

Tesla believed an **alternating** (ALL-ter-nate-ing) **current**, or AC, was a better way to make electricity. It was much safer than direct current. It was also more practical. Electricity could be sent to customers miles away. It could do this with the help of **transformers**. Transformers don't work for DC, or direct current.

Edison disagreed with Tesla. This disagreement got so bad it strained their friendship.

There are many stories about what happened next. Most say that Edison promised to pay Tesla if he could improve Edison's power plants. Tesla made the improvements over the course of a year. Then he asked Edison for his money. Edison said he was only joking and refused to pay. Tesla stormed off and started his own company.

In the end, Tesla had a good idea. Today, all of our electricity is AC, or alternating current.

AC/DC

Lightning is a natural form of electricity. It produces a kind of electrical current called direct current, or DC. This means that the electrons (uh-LEK-tronz) flow in one direction. But if you try to use DC to move electricity from a power plant to a home, it does not work so well. Modern power stations use alternating current, or AC. In AC, the electrons move in one direction and then the other. This makes it easier to move electricity over long distances without losing energy.

AC or DC?

This image shows the lights of present day Prince George, British Columbia. The camera has captured light motion over time. The dots along the light trails visually capture alternating current blinking or alternating. If the current observed was direct current, you would see solid lines of light.

Pioneers of Electromagnetism

Electromagnetism is a powerful force. It is made from the relationship between electricity and magnetism. It is the force behind much of the power we use today.

Many scientists, including Edison, helped to discover the power of electricity and electromagnetism. They also invented ways to put this power to work. The following pages tell about some of their contributions.

Benjamin Franklin, Inventor

Before Thomas Edison, others were curious about the world around them. Benjamin Franklin was one of these curious people. Among other things, Franklin was very interested in electricity.

Franklin lived in America during colonial times. He was born in Boston in 1706. He finished school at a young age and then began working. Franklin held many jobs as he grew older. He was a newspaper editor, merchant, printer, and shopkeeper to name a few. Yet, Franklin became most known as an inventor and politician. The stories behind his inventions are still told today.

Franklin invented many things, including a stove, bifocals, and swim fins. Then, in 1752, Franklin was curious about electricity. He proposed what became a very famous experiment.

Clever Inventor

Have you ever wondered how inventors come up with their ideas? Everyday things can lead to big ideas. One day, Catherine Ryan's wedding ring got stuck on her finger. It made her wonder about nuts and bolts. What if a nut could expand after a bolt was placed inside it? She invented the locking nut to hold bolts in place. Can you think of new uses for everyday things?

It is said that Franklin made a special kite with metal tips. He put a metal key in a glass jar and attached it to the kite string. Then, Franklin tied a silk string to the end of the kite string. He flew the kite in a lightning storm. The metal key was meant to draw the lightning to it. Franklin stood in a nearby shed and held onto the silk string.

Rain wet the string, and it began to conduct electricity! Sparks jumped from the string to the key inside the jar. In this way, Franklin's experiment showed that lightning is a natural form of electricity.

Franklin also invented the **lightning rod**. The lightning rod is a tall piece of iron. It is attached to the top of a building to attract lightning. It provides a direct path for the lightning to the ground. This helps to prevent fires.

What Benjamin Franklin might have looked like while experimenting with electricity in a storm.

▲ Bifocal spectacles were one of Ben Franklin's inventions.

No Patents?

Benjamin Franklin invented many things. However, he never patented any of his own inventions. He wanted to give his inventions to the world for anyone to use. He also founded the American Philosophical Society. It is for people to share their ideas and research.

Oersted's Discovery

Hans Christian Oersted (UR-sted) took Franklin's work a little bit further. He worked for many years to find a link between electricity and **magnetism**.

In 1820, Oersted noticed something strange while setting up an experiment. When he placed a **compass** near an electrical current, the needle moved.

Oersted's discovery proved that electricity could create a magnetic field. It also proved that there is a relationship between electricity and magnetism. His work paved the way for other scientists to investigate electromagnetism.

As Oersted proved, electricity has a direct connection with magnetism.

▲ Hans Christian Oersted

Take a Closer Look

Oersted was born on a small island off the coast of Denmark. Since there was no school on the island, he had to teach himself. Much to his credit, he won a college scholarship.

Ampere's Law

Andre Marie Ampere was a professor from Paris. He was interested in electromagnetism. He described the magnetic force created between two electrical currents. This description is called Ampere's Law. Scientists use Ampere's Law to measure the magnetic field created by an electrical current. The unit of measure is called the **ampere**, or amp.

Did You Know?

Magnets have north and south poles. If you place the north pole of one magnet next to the north pole of another magnet, they will push away from each other. If north and south poles are side-by-side, they will pull toward each other.

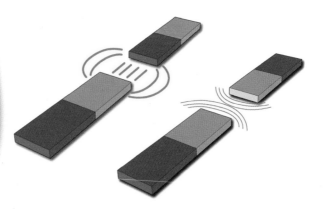

Faraday's Unified Force

Another scientist who studied electromagnetism was Michael Faraday (FAIR-uh-day). In the 1830s, he learned more about how electricity, magnets, and batteries worked.

Faraday figured out how to create magnetic force with electricity. He thought that the power of electricity and magnetism were the same thing. He called it a "single unified force."

Faraday used his idea to build new machines. He built the first electric **motor**, which turned electricity into magnetic forces. The forces made the machine move. He built the first generator, called a dynamo, too. It used moving magnets to make electricity. Faraday is the father of electrical engineering.

Faraday's magnetic spark apparatus

▲ Faraday's Induction Ring Experiment tested electrical currents.

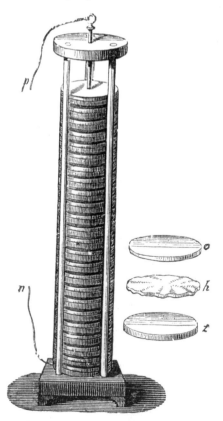

p

n

o

h

z

▲ This is Volta's voltaic pile, built in 1800.

The First Battery

Alessandro Volta created the world's first electric battery in 1799. He learned that he could use the electrical current created by his invention. All he needed to do was connect a wire to it. Volta's name is still used every day. It is used as the unit of measure for the force of an electrical current. This unit is called the **volt**.

Astronomer: Margaret Kivelson

University of California, Los Angeles

Magnetic Moon

Do you like far-out adventure? You might love exploring the solar system. Astronomer Margaret Kivelson does. She has explored Jupiter and other planets.

Kivelson explored Jupiter through the "eyes" and "ears" of a spacecraft called *Galileo*. She used the photographs and information *Galileo* sent back to Earth to study Jupiter's moons. She discovered that Ganymede, Jupiter's biggest moon, acts like a giant magnet. It is surrounded by a magnetic field, just like Earth. This was a big surprise!

Galileo circled Jupiter for seven years before it was destroyed. "It was like saying goodbye to an old friend," says Kivelson.

Galileo was launched ➡ in 1989. It took six years to get to Jupiter, arriving there in 1995.

🔺 Jupiter has over 60 moons! Scientists are especially interested in an icy moon called Europa. They think it might have the ingredients for life to start there.

Kivelson has always liked science. In astronomy, new things are being discovered all the time. "There's so much people had not even dreamed of," she says.

Being There

An astronomer studies space. Kivelson studies how planets and moons affect the space around them. If you were an astronomer you might . . .

- Explore other planets and moons for signs of life.

- Discover new moons or comets.

- Study how the universe began.

- Search for planets outside our solar system.

How Do They Know?
Astronomers study the skies using telescopes and robotic spacecraft such as *Galileo*. They learn about a planet's chemistry by the way the planet sends light. Spacecraft can measure temperatures of a planet or moon. They can also send close-up photographs.

Think About It
If you could explore another planet, which would it be? Why?

Experts Tell Us . . .
"We're still busy studying all the data from *Galileo*," says Kivelson.

Lab: Create an Electromagnet

Electrical currents produce magnetic fields around them. When you make a coil out of conducting wire, you can strengthen the magnetic field. This device is called an **electromagnet**. The more coils of wire, the stronger the magnetic field. You can add a piece of metal, too. This makes the electromagnet even stronger.

Try this.

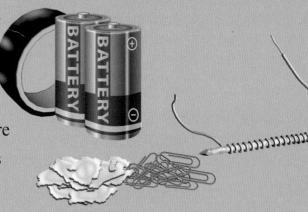

Materials

- a 2-inch iron nail
- heavy, insulated wire
- two D-cell batteries
- 10 paper clips
- scraps of paper
- masking tape

Procedure

1 Wrap 20 turns of wire around the nail.

2 Leave about 8 inches of wire hanging from each end of the coil around the nail.

3 Peel back 3 inches of the insulating material from each end of the wire.

4 Tape the positive end of one D-cell battery to the negative end of the second battery.

5 Tape one end of the wire to the positive end of the batteries and one end to the negative end of the batteries.

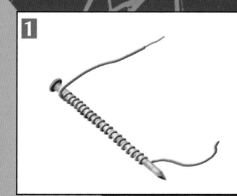

6 Make a pile of paper clips and a pile of paper scraps.

7 Run the nail with the coiled wire over the paper clips and the scraps of paper. Observe what happens.

8 Try steps 1 through 7 again, but this time coil the wire tighter in step 2. Create an electromagnet with 50 turns around the nail.

9 Make another pile of paper clips.

10 Run the nail with the coiled wire over the paper clips. Observe what happens.

11 Record your results.

Extension

What makes a better electromagnet: more electricity or more coils around the nail? Create an experiment to find out.

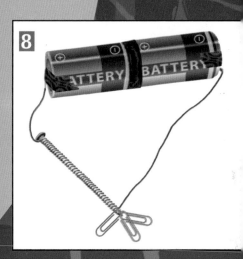

Try using materials other than the nail. Try a pencil. Try a pen. Try a crayon. Do they work? How well? Why do you think this is so?

Glossary

alkaline—a type of battery made of a neutral chemical substance

alternating current (AC)—an electrical current in which the electrons move one way, then the other

ampere (amp)—the unit of measure for a current

compass—a device used to determine direction (north, south, east, west)

current—the flow of electricity through a conductor

direct current (DC)—an electrical current in which the electrons move in one direction

electrical engineer—a person in the branch of engineering that deals with the technology of electricity, especially the design and application of circuitry and equipment for power generation and distribution

electrician—one whose occupation is the installation, maintenance, repair, or operation of electric equipment and circuitry

electricity—a form of energy

electromagnet—a device formed by coiling wire around a metal such as iron, then passing an electrical current through the wire to create a magnet

electromagnetism—magnetism produced by an electric current

generator—a machine that changes mechanical energy into electrical energy

invention—an original device

lightning rod—a metallic conductor that is attached to a high point and leads to the ground; protects the building from destruction by lightning

magnetism—the property of magnets that allow them to attract iron

Morse code—a series of dots and dashes used to send messages

motor—a machine that changes electrical or chemical energy into mechanical energy

patent—a document that gives an inventor the right to be the only person who sells his or her invention

telegraph—an electrical device used to send messages over a wire

transformer—a device used to step up and down voltage so that AC electricity can be transmitted over distances

volt—the unit of measure for the force of an electrical current; unit of measure of voltage

Index

alkaline, 4

alternating current (AC), 16–17

American Philosophical Society, 21

ampere (amp), 23

Ampere, Andre Marie, 23

compass, 22–23

current, 11, 15–17, 22–25, 28–29

direct current (DC), 14–17

Edison, Thomas, 4–19

electrical engineer, 9, 13, 24

electrician, 13

electricity, 4–7, 12–25

electromagnet, 28–29

electromagnetism, 18, 22–25

Faraday, Michael, 24–25

Franklin, Benjamin, 18–21

Galileo, 26–27

Ganymede, 26

General Electric, 12

generator, 12, 24

Henry, Beulah, 11

inventions, 4–5, 8–11, 18–21, 24–25

Jupiter, 26–27

Kivelson, Margaret, 26–27

Kies, Mary Dixon, 5

Kiley, Mattie "Ma," 7

light bulb, 4, 10–11

lightning rod, 20–21

magnetism, 18, 22–25

Morse code, 7

motor, 24

Ochoa, Ellen, 9

Oersted, Hans Christian, 22–23

patent, 5, 9, 11, 14, 21

phonograph, 4, 8–9

Ryan, Catherine, 19

Tesla, Nikola, 14–16

telegraph, 6–7, 15

transformer, 16

volt, 25

Volta, Alessandro, 25

Wizard of Menlo Park, 4–5

Sally Ride Science™ is an innovative content company dedicated to fueling young people's interests in science. Our publications and programs provide opportunities for students and teachers to explore the captivating world of science—from astrobiology to zoology. We bring science to life and show young people that science is creative, collaborative, fascinating, and fun.

Image Credits